*to*

_____

*from*

_____

# The Simple Truths of
# APPRECIATION

*How each of us can choose to make a difference*

Barbara A. Glanz

Cover Photo: Masterfile

Many thanks to these photographers whose images appear in this book:
Rich Nickel (www.richnickeldesign.com): pages 34, 38, 44, 52, 58, 62, 68, 72, 76, 78
Steve Terrill (www.steveterrill.com): pages 18, 29, 37, 42
Bruce Heinemann (www.theartofnature.com): pages 8, 57
Ken Jenkins (www.kenjenkins.com): page 50
Todd Reed (www.toddreedphoto.com): page 30

Editor: Julie Kellogg

Published by Simple Truths, an imprint of Sourcebooks, Inc.
P.O. Box 4410, Naperville, Illinois 60567-4410
(630) 961-3900
Fax: (630) 961-2168
www.sourcebooks.com

Printed and bound in China.
OGP 10 9 8 7 6 5 4 3 2

# CONTENTS

"I can go for **2** months **on 1** compliment."

— MARK TWAIN

M any years ago William James said, "The deepest principle of human nature is a craving to be appreciated."

I truly believe that the *need to be validated and appreciated* as a worthwhile human being is greater than ever before, especially in our schools and our workplaces.

A recent study indicated that last year 65% of our workforce reported they had received NO appreciation for the good work they had done!

Without purpose, passion, and a sense that we are making a difference, what meaning does our life really have, and why should we strive to do our best work? The beauty of appreciation is that we can each *give it to anyone we choose.* It costs nothing, except a few moments of our time.

YOU NEVER KNOW WHEN A MOMENT AND A FEW SINCERE WORDS CAN HAVE AN IMPACT ON A LIFE.

— ZIG ZIGLAR

*Consider this example:*

One snowy February day I walked into the Ladies washroom at O'Hare Airport. There was a woman there who was cleaning. She was all hunched over, glum-looking, and listlessly going through the motions of her job. I walked over, gently touched her on the arm, looked her directly in the eyes, and said,

**"Thank you so much for keeping this washroom clean. You're really making a difference for all of us who travel."**

She stopped what she was doing, looked at me with wonder in her eyes, immediately straightened up, and began cleaning with a passion. A huge smile spread across her face, and by the time I left, she was passing out towels to all the women who were washing their hands!

I left that washroom with tears in my eyes because *that interaction had cost me nothing.* However, it changed her life, at least for a few moments. My appreciation of her and the value of her very important work gave her a purpose and a reason for being. SHE WAS MAKING A DIFFERENCE!

When I work with an organization, I often spend a day there. As I walk around the building, I ask people, "What is your work?" Most often they give me either a job title or a job description. What I then say to them is this: *"Every one of us in this world is so much MORE than a title or a job description. When I ask you, 'What is your work?', what I want you to think about is:*

HOW IS WHAT YOU DO
EVERY DAY
MAKING SOMEONE'S
LIFE BETTER?

*It does not matter whether you clean the restrooms or run the company, you can find a way to make someone's life better, and THAT is your very important work!"*

As I share this idea, I see people's faces light up because at last they realize that they DO make a difference, and their work IS important.

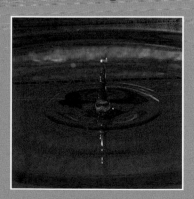 They feel appreciated because they are making the world a better place.

Each one of us can help people in the world around us…whether it is in our workplace, our home, or as we go through the daily interactions of our lives…to feel appreciated and valuable.

*Appreciation is a* FREE *gift* that you can give to anyone you encounter — it is completely your choice. And each time you choose to thank someone for a job well done, you are making the world a better place.

This quotation from Mother Teresa sums up the

way I choose to live my life:

"BE KIND AND
MERCIFUL.
LET NO ONE EVER COME
TO YOU WITHOUT COMING
AWAY BETTER AND
HAPPIER."

*THAT* is the gift of appreciation!

# THE TEACHER STORY—
## The Life-changing
## Gift of Appreciation

In my keynote speeches and workshops, CARE is an acronym I use for the elements of a caring, creative, joyful (and more productive!) workplace and home. The "A" in CARE stands for **"Appreciation for All."**

As I speak about Appreciation, I use one of my favorite quotations from Albert Schweitzer. ▸

"SOMETIMES OUR LIGHT GOES OUT BUT IS BLOWN AGAIN INTO FLAME BY AN ENCOUNTER WITH ANOTHER HUMAN BEING. EACH OF US OWES THE DEEPEST THANKS TO THOSE WHO HAVE REKINDLED THIS INNER LIGHT."

Then I ask my audiences to please shut their eyes and think about someone who, at some time in their lives, has rekindled their inner light. I leave the room in silence for several minutes, and it is always a profound experience for everyone as they

*remember the* JOY they received from being appreciated by someone when they needed it the most.

Afterwards, I ask them to write down the name of the person they thought of and to commit to their own act of appreciation by letting that person know in the next 72 hours that he or she was thought of. I suggest a phone call, a note, or even a little prayer if they are no longer living.

After one very moving session, a gentleman came up to talk with me and thanked me for creating a new awareness in him. He said he had thought of his eighth grade literature teacher because she was everyone's favorite teacher, and had really made a difference in all of their lives. He planned to track her down and let me know what happened.

One afternoon nearly two and a half months later, I received a call from him. He was choked up on the phone and could hardly get through his story. He said that it had taken him nearly two months to track his teacher down, and when he finally found her, he wrote to her.

The following week he received this letter: ▸

Dear John,

You will never know how ~~much~~
me. I am 83 years old, an~~d~~
one room. My friends a~~re~~

I taught for 50 years an~~d~~
you" letter I have ever g~~otten~~
Sometimes I wonder w~~ho~~
read and reread your le~~tter~~

uch your letter meant to

am living all alone in

ll gone. My family's gone.

ours is the first "thank

en from a student.

t I did with my life. I will

r until the day I die.

He just sobbed on the phone. He said, "She is always the one we talk about at every reunion. She was everyone's favorite teacher – we *loved* her!"  But, **no one had ever told her**… until she received his letter.

Dear Reader,

My wish for each of you is that you will be changed after reading this book; that you will

## *become more loving and appreciative*

as you go through your daily lives. You can see from this "every man's" story the life-changing gift we can each give by simply sharing our appreciation with those around us.

APPRECIATION IS A
WONDERFUL THING: IT MAKES
WHAT IS EXCELLENT IN OTHERS
BELONG TO US AS WELL.

— VOLTAIRE

# The Simple Truths of
# APPRECIATION

*Ten things you need to remember*

# ~1 The Simple Truths of Appreciation

# EVERYONE
## WANTS
### *and*
## NEEDS IT

No matter who we are or what our actions may say, we all want to be recognized and appreciated. I often quote Lou Holtz, the famous Notre Dame coach, who said, "Why is it that the people who need love, (appreciation), and understanding the most usually deserve it the least?"

Jaime Escalante, the teacher on whom the movie *Stand and Deliver* was based, tells an amazing story about a mistaken identity and the difference it made in a young man's life.

This teacher had two students in his class who were both named Johnny. One Johnny was an excellent student, a happy child, and always had his homework completed on time. The other Johnny was always in trouble, never had his work finished, and generally made the teacher's life miserable.

The night of their first PTA Open House of the year a mother stayed after the meeting to ask about her son, Johnny, and how he was getting along in the class. Assuming it was the mother of the "good" Johnny, the teacher replied, "I can't tell you how much I appreciate him. I am so glad he's in my class."

The next day, for the first time all year, the "problem" Johnny had all his work done, he spoke up in class, and never once caused a disruption. He even volunteered to help another student. The teacher was astounded!

At the end of the day when everyone else had left, "problem" Johnny came up to the teacher and said, "My Mom told me what you said about me last night. *I haven't ever had a teacher who wanted me in his class."*

Reprinted with permission from *CARE Packages for the Home,* Barbara A. Glanz, 1998.

That Johnny became one of the best students the teacher ever had – and all because of a mistaken dose of appreciation! No matter who we are and what our situation in life is, we all need to be appreciated.

WHEREVER
THERE IS A
HUMAN BEING,
THERE IS AN OPPORTUNITY
FOR KINDNESS.

# IT DOESN'T HAVE *to be* SOMETHING "BIG"

My friend, Bob Danzig, has an amazing story. Simple words of appreciation and encouragement changed his life. Bob was in five foster homes during his youth, and said he spent his childhood trying to find someone to love and appreciate him.

When he was nine years old, he had a new social worker. He said after she had done all the paperwork to move him to yet another foster home, she sat him down, looked him directly in the eyes, and said, "Bobby, I want you to always remember these words: YOU ARE WORTHWHILE!"

Bob says that no one had ever said anything like that to him, and each time they met, she repeated those words. They became an affirmation of appreciation that he heard over and over again in his head.

Bob graduated at sixteen, not because he was smart, he says, but because he got mixed up in the system!  He soon took a job at the *Albany New York Times* as a copy boy, and his very first boss was a woman named Margaret.

After he had worked there about six months, Margaret called him into her office one day and asked him to sit down. He thought for sure he was going to be fired! She looked him right in the eyes and said to him, "I have been the office manager for 15 years — I have been observing you — and I believe YOU ARE FULL OF PROMISE." Those words, on that day, gave him permission to aspire.

Those two positive messages of appreciation played over and over again in his head and ultimately gave him the courage to be the very best he could be. Sixteen years later he became the Publisher of the *Albany New York Times,* and seven years after that, he became CEO of Hearst Newspapers, one of the largest newspaper companies in the world—

## *and he credits it all to those simple words of appreciation and love.*

What a wonderful example of how little gifts of appreciation can make such a difference in a life!

The happiness of life
is made up of minute fractions –
the little soon forgotten charities
of a kiss or smile, a kind look,
a heartfelt compliment,
and the countless infinitesimals
of pleasurable and genial feeling.

– SAMUEL TAYLOR COLERIDGE

*3 The Simple Truths of Appreciation*

# MAKE IT
## PERSONAL

Think of special ways you can appreciate others that will touch their lives in a personal way. These gifts are especially meaningful when they are given for no special reason except to show that you care about them, and you appreciate their presence in your life. I call these "angel gifts" because they always seem to come at a time when you need them most.

The most special "angel gift" I have ever received came when I desperately needed encouragement, appreciation, and love. When our third child, Erin, was born, Garrett was seven and Gretchen was two and a half. Just six weeks after her birth, my husband, Charlie, hurt his back and was completely immobilized, leaving the full responsibility of caring for him, the house, a new baby, and the other children to me.

During the first week he was in bed, I (Super Mom in action!) was boiling water very late one night to make Easter eggs for the children to color the next day, since it was Easter weekend. At the same time, I was talking on the phone with a friend.

Cradling the phone between my ear and my chin, I carried the pot of eggs and boiling water over to the sink. While pouring the hot water out, and trying to carry on a conversation at the same time, I accidentally dumped the boiling water all over my forearm, causing third degree burns. Because it was very late, and Charlie was unable to move, I even had to drive myself to the emergency room!

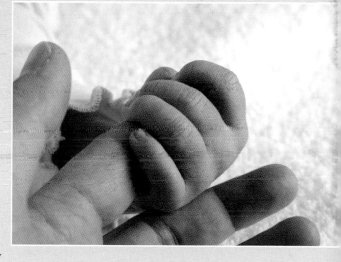

Can you imagine what my life was like trying to take care of a new baby, an injured husband, and two other young children—with a badly burned arm? Since my mother was unable to come to help, I had a neighbor who came in each day to bathe the baby and another friend who came over to change my bandages twice a day.

In the midst of all this, the doctors decided that Charlie needed surgery, so he was taken to the hospital for a laminectomy. Now, I was not only trying to care for a house and three young children, but also be at the hospital to support Charlie, and still breastfeed a seven and a half week old baby! On top of everything else, this was a difficult time for us financially because I had chosen to postpone my career and stay home with the children, and Charlie's was our only income.

In those days we used cotton diapers which needed to be washed several times a week. It was an extremely time-consuming and unpleasant task! (Young people today probably don't even remember cotton diapers.)

Several days after Charlie's surgery, I returned home from the hospital very late one night, completely exhausted and nearly in tears. On the front porch step sat a huge round plastic hamper filled with three dozen sparkling white diapers tied in a large plastic bag, and a note which read: ▶

"The Edward Burkeen family has given you the gift of diaper service for one month. Please put the dirty diapers in this hamper, and we will pick it up and bring you a new supply of fresh diapers twice a week for the next four weeks. They want you to know how much they appreciate all you are doing for your family, and they hope this will help make your life a bit easier."

At that moment I truly felt that I did have a guardian angel. Never, ever, will I forget the compassion, appreciation, and encouragement that those dear friends gave me during a most difficult time in my life.

To whom might you give an **"angel gift"** of appreciation today?

50

YOU
WHO ARE LETTING…
YOUR FRIEND'S HEART ACHE
FOR A WORD OF
APPRECIATION
OR SYMPATHY…
…WHICH YOU MEAN
TO GIVE HIM
SOMEDAY…
THE TIME IS SHORT!

– PHILLIPS BROOKS

# 4 The Simple Truths of Appreciation

# BE
## CREATIVE

**H**ow do you appreciate others around you? Get your creative juices going to determine some unusual, attention-getting, delightful ways you can thank others in your life. Consider leaving special post-it notes, affirming stickers, handwritten notes of any kind or bringing a picnic lunch to share with someone, and of course, people love any kind of treats.

A friend recently sent a business colleague the following huge 3-D "treat" card with each of the candies glued onto a poster board amidst the words:

You are **CERTS**tainly a **LIFESAVER** and worth **$100,000** to us! Sometimes life is a **ROCKY ROAD** but **BAR NONE,** you are always **MOUNDS** of **JOY**, laughs, and **SNICKERS**! You are a **BOUNTY** of fun, very **CAREFREE**, and **EXTRA** special. **SKOR** big and count down to **PAYDAY.** Best wishes, **HUGS,** and **KISSES!**

My friend, Dick Bruso, from Denver, Colorado, tells of a wonderfully creative way he showed appreciation towards his precious wife.

Dick said, *"A couple of years ago, shortly before Father's Day, Jenny, one of my four grown daughters asked me what I wanted for Father's Day, since 'Dads are hard to buy for!' For once, I had an immediate answer. Earlier that month, my wife, Joann, and I had visited an upscale women's clothing store where my youngest daughter, Joy, was working as a sales associate. For the fun of it, my wife decided to try on some expensive outfits, including a beautiful brown and gold silk dress that looked absolutely fabulous on her.*

*Although I could see how much she liked it, we both realized it was a lot more than we could afford. Thus, when my daughter asked me what I wanted for Father's Day, I suggested that all my daughters consider pooling their resources in order to buy "me" that dress for Father's Day. And that's exactly what they did!*

*When our family gathered together on Father's Day to celebrate, my four daughters (Julie-ann, Jackie, Jenny, and Joy) presented me with my gift, wrapped, of course, in a manly looking gift-box. When I opened it, much to my wife's absolute surprise and delight, there was that special dress that she had wanted.*

*Since then, I have had the pleasure on numerous occasions of seeing my lovely wife light up a room wearing my favorite Father's Day gift. What a blessing it has been and what a special way to show my appreciation for her love and caring through all these years!"*

What a creative way to appreciate someone – by sacrificing your desires for someone you love, on YOUR special day.

# There are two things that people want more than sex and money – recognition and praise.

— MARY KAY ASH, CEO, MARY KAY COSMETICS

~5 *The Simple Truths of Appreciation*

SURPRISE
PEOPLE
IF YOU CAN

A heartwarming story in *The Oregonian* told of how a mail carrier's 47th birthday was celebrated by all of his customers. Fred Wilkins, a mail carrier for the U.S. Postal Service, was surprised on his birthday by the Cedar Hills residents whom he had served for 13 years. One of the neighbors said, "Everyone loves this man. He walks 12 miles a day to take care of his people." His customers tied balloons to mail boxes, posted "Happy Birthday" signs, decorated Wilkins' truck and lavished him with gifts. What a wonderful birthday surprise from appreciative customers. He, of course, has never forgotten it.

One of my clients shared how they surprised and appreciated the custodial person in their building. They knew the next day was his birthday, so before everyone left that night, they emptied their own wastebaskets. Then they drew a circle the size of the bottom of the can and cut it out. On it they each printed a message such as "Happy Birthday, John! We appreciate your hard work for us" and placed it in their wastebaskets. That night, when the custodian came on shift at midnight, he found NO wastebaskets to empty in the entire building, and every one had a personal message just for him. He says he will NEVER forget that day! (Nor will the rest of the employees as they learned to appreciate him even more when they had to clean up after themselves…)

IT IS GOOD TO APPRECIATE THAT LIFE IS NOW.
WHATEVER IT OFFERS, LITTLE OR MUCH,
LIFE IS NOW –
THIS DAY – THIS HOUR.

— CHARLES MACOMB FLANDRAU

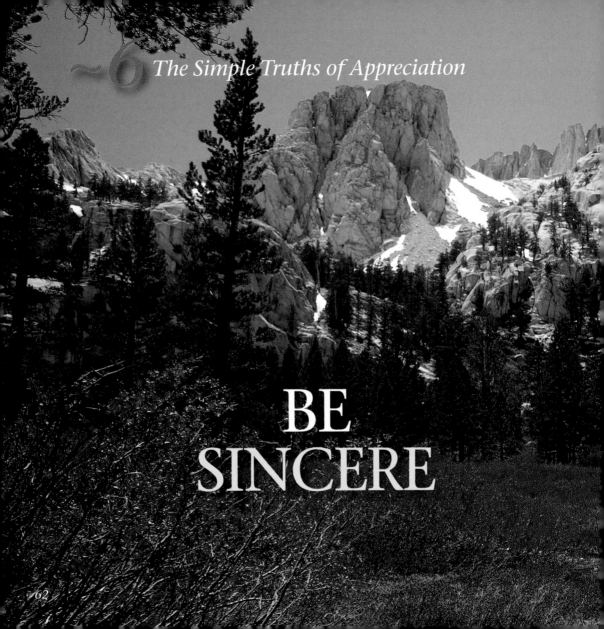

# BE
# SINCERE

Several years ago my husband of nearly 34 years died of cancer. Soon after, I moved from Illinois to Florida where I knew only five people. For the first year and a half I nearly died of loneliness and often came home to my empty condo in tears.

After one particularly bad day, I drove into my parking space and hit the pole next to my car. I dented the side of the car and left a large strip of white paint down the side. At that point in my life I didn't have anyone nearby I could call for help, so I felt totally and completely alone.

Hardly able to see through my tears, I managed to get into the elevator and up to my apartment, wondering if anyone in the world really cared about me. When I went to open the door, however, I saw a small package wedged between the screen and the storm door. When I opened it, I was amazed to find a beautiful silver necklace with an amethyst pendant. It was from Keith Cotham, a young man who was in one of my training sessions years before. The only communications we ever had were the quarterly newsletters I sent to all my clients, and a Christmas card each year.

His note said that he had been thinking of me and the difference I had made in his life. He just wanted to *send me a little gift of his appreciation.* When he saw the necklace, it reminded him of me, and he hoped it would bring me some of the joy I had brought into his life.

I was deeply touched, as there was absolutely no reason for him to send me a gift, and yet the sincerity of his appreciation was one of the most precious treasures I have ever received.

*Is there someone in your past
who could use your appreciation today?*

"People want to be appreciated, not impressed. They want to be regarded as human beings, not as mere sounding boards for other people's egos.

They want to be treated as an end in themselves, not as a means toward the gratification of another's vanity."

— SYDNEY J. HARRIS

*The Simple Truths of Appreciation*

# HAVE
## A PLAN

I have found that I often need to have a plan to make sure that I remember to appreciate people in the midst of my busy life of speaking, writing, and travel. I have chosen Wednesday as my "A" day. No matter where I am in the world, I do not go to bed until I have thanked or appreciated at least one person in a special way — by phoning, sending an e-mail message, writing a note, sending a little gift, or telling them in person. Although I try to appreciate people every single day, this plan helps me to focus on **the importance of saying "Thank you" on a consistent basis.**

Other people keep a large letter "A" on their desks or in their kitchen as a reminder to appreciate others. Recently, I made a conscious decision not to think something nice about someone without actually telling them. It is amazing to see how people light up when you really notice them and the wonderful, caring things they do.

Another idea is to put five pennies in your right pocket at the beginning of each day. Then, whenever you appreciate someone during the day, move one penny to your left pocket. Your goal is that by the end of the day, you will have moved all the pennies to the other side — and best of all, you will have made five people very happy!

Find something that works for you — and then DO it!

# EVERY CHARITABLE ACT IS A STEPPING STONE TOWARD HEAVEN.

— Henry Ward Beecher

# SHARE YOURSELF – FROM THE HEART

When we truly think of others and what we can do just for them, our appreciation becomes *a selfless gift of love.*

One of my most memorable and heartfelt gifts of appreciation came from my younger brother, Brian Bauerle. He was living in Kansas City at the time, having just graduated from the University of Kansas, and was serving as Executive Director of the National Child Abuse Foundation. I was a stay-at-home Mom with three young children, we were on a limited budget, and rarely was there ever time, or money, for me to do something "just for me."

Brian was coming to Chicago for meetings and called to say that he was going to stay an extra day or two, and he had a surprise planned for his "big Sis." He said I was to call a baby-sitter to come for the whole day, I was to dress up in my best outfit, and take the train downtown and meet him for lunch. Then Charlie (my husband) was to join us after work for a special dinner — all on him!

At lunch Brian announced that "we were going shopping to look for a wonderful new dress" in appreciation for what a great sister, Mom, and wife I was. I will never forget my absolute delight shopping at all the "best" downtown stores, trying on beautiful dresses, and then coming out for Brian's approval.

Since Charlie didn't like to shop, I rarely had the experience of having a man along. It was fun watching all the sales ladies give us extra attention in anticipation of us spending more money. I really felt like a princess!

We finally found a bright red dress (my favorite color) that was simply made for me. It was much more expensive than I ever could have afforded, but Brian bought it for me. Years later, even though it is nearly worn out, I cannot bear to throw that dress away because of the memories of Brian's precious gift.

What amazes me the most is that he was a very young, single man at the time; yet he somehow knew what could touch a young mother's heart and spirit in an unforgettable way. Thank you, Brian, for appreciating me and making me feel so special *at a time when I needed it the most!*

When you appreciate from your heart, truly giving of yourself, you touch people in ways they will never forget.

"We have a duty to
encourage one another.
Many a time a word of praise
or thanks or appreciation
or cheer has kept a
man on his feet.
Blessed is the man who
speaks such a word."

— WILLIAM BARCLAY

# MAKE IT
## MEMORABLE

Tim Richardson, a speaker friend, shared that he saw the most incredible example of appreciation on a Delta flight last year: "It was the captain's last flight and his wife, a flight attendant, coordinated a most unbelievable onboard party for him...balloons at the gate as we boarded, cake and champagne on the flight for everyone, a guest book which all the passengers signed, and even free prizes during the flight. When we landed, the Salt Lake City Police Department escorted the plane to the gate and the Fire Department shot their hoses in the air for us to drive through. I will never forget that day, and I am sure neither will the Captain!"

After I had spoken to a large manufacturing company, a gentleman came up to me afterwards and told me that he had the lowest performing team in the whole company. He said they had never met their goals once...but that I had gotten him thinking.

Ten months later he called me late one afternoon, and from the ecstatic tone in his voice, I knew something wonderful had happened!

He said that after I was there, he got his whole team together and said to them, "If any of you meet your goals this quarter, *I'm going to call your mothers!*"

As a result of that challenge, EVERY SINGLE ONE of them met their goals for the first time ever…And he said making the calls was one of the nicest experiences he had ever had. Some of the mothers even cried after hearing what their son or daughter had achieved.

I believe no matter how old we are, we are left with unforgettable memories when someone takes the time to call our parent, spouse, or significant other to tell them how much they appreciate us, and to thank them for us and our good work.

When we do something unusual to appreciate someone, we create a memory that will last forever.

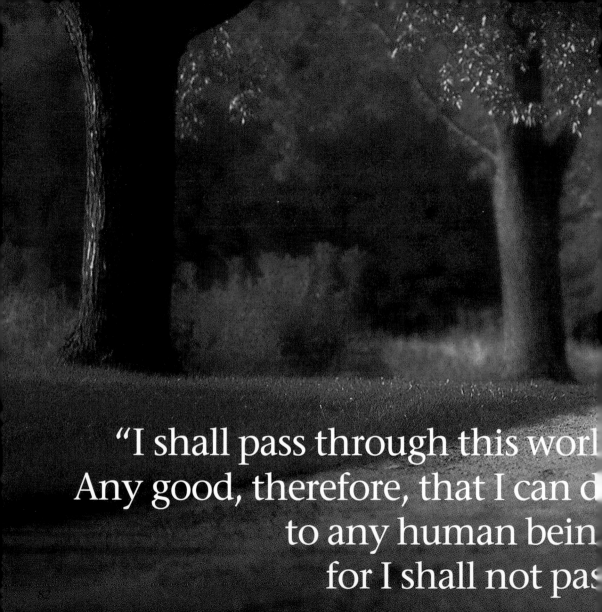

"I shall pass through this worl
Any good, therefore, that I can d
to any human bein
for I shall not pas

ut once.

r any kindness I can show

et me do it now...

his way again."

— Etienne de Grellet

# YOU WILL RECEIVE MORE THAN YOU GIVE

M ike Hall of Englewood, Colorado, feels that children need to receive more appreciation and positive messages of affirmation, so this is a fax he sent to his daughter, Carly, from his office downtown:

**FAX**

Dear Carly,

I just wanted to tell you how TERRIFIC you look today. I am so proud to be your father. You are a wonderful daughter, and you make Mom and me the happiest parents in the entire solar system.

Please save a kiss for me—and give your Mom a big smooch too. I love you guys forever and ever.

Let's do something fun after work today—OK?

Love, Dad

This was Carly's reply:

Dear Dad,
I would Love
to go somewhere fun
to night!! I gave mom
a big smooch. I will
do the same to you.
You look TERRIFIC
today too!! how
are you doing at
work today. write
back ✱ soon!!!!!!!!!!
Love,
Carly
Hall

Mike will never forget this precious gift from his little girl.

My friend, Kevin Eikenberry tells about an experience he had that gave him special joy:

**I was boarding a flight in Edmonton, Alberta, bound for Toronto after a long day. As I handed my boarding pass to the Air Canada gate agent, I asked her if she was having a good day. She looked at me, smiled, and said, "All the better for you asking me, thanks."**

**As I literally skipped down the jet way, I smiled. I have asked hundreds of people if they are having a good day. Never have I received that response. I've heard, "It's OK," "No, not really," and "Fine, thanks." But never, until now, have I heard, "All the better for you asking me, thanks."**

**Her response was gracious and warm. It wowed me as a customer – giving me a very positive experience with Air Canada even before I was on the plane! More importantly, it made me feel special as a human being. What would have been a normal flight was changed by eight words – words I will never forget.**

When we reach out to celebrate and appreciate others, we will always receive more than we give. The Bible tells us, "It is more blessed to give than to receive," and in every instance in my life I have found this to be absolutely true.

"THE MOST ATTRACTIVE PEOPLE IN THE WORLD ARE THE ONES WHO ARE INTERESTED IN OTHERS – TURNED OUTWARD IN CHEERFULNESS, KINDNESS, APPRECIATION, INSTEAD OF TURNED INWARD TO BE CONSTANTLY CENTERED IN THEMSELVES."

— PAT BOONE

## CONCLUSION

My wonderful friend, David Roth, has written a song about appreciation. It's a true story, and I wonder how many of us will be moved to an action of appreciation because of it:

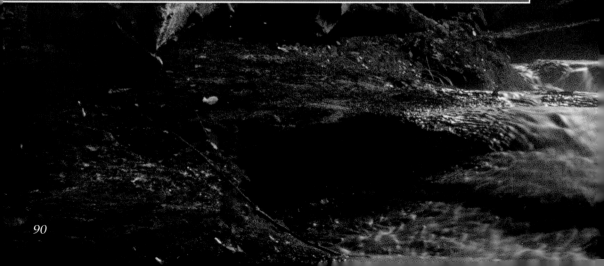

# THANK YOU MR. RYAN

The first time I heard that song was a time I well remember
It all goes back some 20 years to Mr. Ryan's classroom
One day he brought his old guitar and sang his favorite songs for us
And the single one that I remember most was "All My Trials"

Something in his simple singing touched my very 6th-grade soul
The harmonies he taught us are the ones that I still know today
The verse about the "Tree of Life" was wondrous to a 12-year old
And many times these twenty years I've wished that I could say:

Thank you for the music, Mr. Ryan
The simple gift you gave that day is one I've treasured dearly
I'll always see you sitting up there singing "All My Trials"
You'll never know how much it's meant to me

*W*ent home to see my folks in June, the town that I grew up in
Three of us were sitting in the kitchen having coffee
I mentioned Mr. Ryan, how I wondered what became of him
Mother said she'd heard that he's still working at my school

*I* grabbed my coat and ran outside, retracing old familiar routes
The shortcut through the playground and the echo of that hallway
And there he was in room eleven, wiping off the blackboard
I took a breath and cleared my throat and stepped back into time:

*T*hank you for the music Mr. Ryan
The simple gift you gave that day is one I've treasured dearly
I'll always see you sitting up there singing "All My Trials"
You'll never know how much it's meant to me

*We sat and talked for quite a while, I don't think that he remembered me*

*But I told him of my work and where I've been and what I've done*

*And finally he leaned back and said, "It's amazing that you come today*

*Just last night my mother and I were talking until one*

*She asked me was I happy, I said 'yes, I love my teaching*

*But I'm sad I never married, that I never fathered children . . .'*

*'Oh yes,' she said, 'oh yes, my son, you've fathered several hundred .'*

*And now I look across my cluttered desk, and here you've come*

*Thank you for the visit, my dear child*

*The simple gift you gave today is one I'll treasure dearly*

*I'll always see you sitting up here filling in these 20 years*

*You'll never know how much it's meant to me*

*You'll never know how much it's meant to me"*

## ABOUT THE AUTHOR

 Barbara Glanz, one of fewer than 500 Certified Speaking Professionals worldwide, works with organizations that want to improve morale, retention, and service and with people who want to rediscover the joy in their work and in their lives. Using her Master's degree in Adult Learning, she has spoken on 7 continents and in all 50 states to organizations as diverse as Nordstrom, Honda, the Nat'l. Association for Employee Recognition, Southwest Airlines, Bank of America, USAA, Kaiser Permanente, Hallmark, the US Dept. of Energy, Shangri-La Hotels, Merry Maids, Verizon, and the Singapore Security Police!

Known as the business speaker who speaks to your heart as well as to your head, she lives and breathes her personal motto, "Spreading Contagious Enthusiasm.™" She is the author of eleven books, including *The Simple Truths of Service,* co-authored with Ken Blanchard; *What Can I Do? Ideas to Help Those Who Have Experienced Loss; Balancing Acts; CARE Packages for the Workplace; CARE Packages for the Home;* and *CARE Packages for your Customers.* She lives on the beach in Sarasota, Florida, and adores her three grandchildren, Gavin, Kinsey, and Owen.

For more information, visit www.barbaraglanz.com. Barbara can be reached at 941-312-9169; Fax 941-349-8209; or by email at bglanz@barbaraglanz.com.